CHRISTIANS CONTEMPLATING **ABORTION**?

She is full of fear for her future and how she thought it would look like.

Proverbs 31:25 reads "Strength and honour are her clothing and she will rejoice in time to come."

SHARON MCFEE

Ark House Press
PO Box 1722, Port Orchard, WA 98366 USA
PO Box 1321, Mona Vale NSW 1660 Australia
PO Box 318 334, West Harbour, Auckland 0661 New Zealand
arkhousepress.com

Some names and identifying details have been changed to protect the privacy of individuals.

Cataloguing in Publication Data:
Title: Christian's Contemplating Abortion?
ISBN: 978-0-6488873-1-7 (pbk)
Other Authors/Contributors: McFee, Sharon

Design by initiateagency.com

INTRODUCTION

Following on from my autobiography "Reconciled from abortion's chains" comes this book "Christians contemplating abortion?"

It was prophesied to me through the pastor of the church I was a part of, that another book was coming which the Lord wanted me to write. That same night I woke up and I was acutely aware of what many single Christian women were feeling having just discovered that they were indeed expecting a baby and the full range of emotions and thoughts swirling around their minds in confusion, at this vulnerable time. You see, I once was a young, single 18 year old woman who found out she was to become a mother.

My prayer is that this book will find itself in the hands of the grandmothers and mothers of these vulnerable young women who find themselves in this situation to persuade and direct them onto the path of life.

CHAPTER 1

Deuteronomy 30:19
I call heaven and earth to witness against you today, that
I have set before you life and death, blessing and curse.
Therefore choose life, that you and your offspring may live.

Life is a gift, given by God. The percentage rate of unprotected sex producing a conception in human beings is actually pretty low even for healthy fertile young couples. So many couples are simply not able to conceive due to a wide range of reasons e.g. exposure to chemicals in your everyday world; stress; low sperm count for the men; irregular menstrual cycles for the women. Life is precious. You, the reader, have life, and it is to be valued.

Emotions run very high when the woman first finds out that she has missed her period and she takes a pregnancy test. Especially so if she and her husband/partner have not planned or desired it and it has taken them by surprise. We like everything to be in our control and in our timing and, unexpectedly, our lives are turned upside down. Immediate thoughts may turn to "there goes our holiday" "little Chloe is going to school next year and I finally have some time to myself" or "my last pregnancy was a nightmare with constant nausea, even vomiting, the entire 9 months" or "I still remember the labour I went through and how much pain I experienced" to name just a few. Of course, if the woman is unmarried, or just broken up with her partner, or if she is in an abusive or unloving relationship, then carrying the pregnancy full-term becomes more daunting and serious. Every woman who finds herself pregnant, whatever the situation, will look ahead to her future at this crucial point in time to count the cost: to her physical body, her emotional and mental health and well-being, and her past experience in life. All these have a bearing on her outlook. Did her parents accept and welcome her as a baby into the world; did they value her and protect her, or was she rejected and unloved and unwelcomed, which she recognised either consciously or unconsciously. An unexpected pregnancy takes courage, whether for the first time or for the third or fourth time.

Generally, as a rule, every pregnancy is different and every childbirth is different; usually with the first childbirth taking the longest as the uterine muscles come into action, designed as they were by God, and subsequent labours taking somewhat less, as was the case in my situation yet my first and fifth labours took exactly the same length of time of 14 hours.

Our thinking, in the very early part of a woman's pregnancy, can be faulty and emotionally charged as the hormones increase in our bodies, particularly hCG. Some women are more sensitive to those shifting hormones, not to mention the absolute fatigue a women feels in the 1st trimester. The hCG rises sharply in the 1st trimester then dips and levels off around 4 months of pregnancy stage. This is all to be expected and is perfectly normal and can be a time in a woman's life like no other when she feels like a woman in the fullest sense of the word. It is exhilarating, yet scary, with regards to how the future will look and the unknown. I loved the part of pregnancy where I felt I carried "a secret" many people did not know I had a little person inside of me with his/her own DNA and set of 26 chromosomes: eye colour, hair colour, skin colour, genetic strengths and weaknesses – a miracle in fact! A person! God releases His spirit into this new little person at the moment of conception. This new little being is even assigned angels from God. In Matthew 18:10 we read "See that you do not despise one of these little ones. For I tell you that their angels in heaven always see the face of my Father in heaven."

1. Were you caught off guard when you discovered you were expecting a baby?
2. Did you easily fall pregnant?
3. What were your immediate thoughts?

CHAPTER 2

Isaiah 38:19

The living, the living, he thanks you...

In this portion of scripture it talks about King Hezekiah who became sick to the point of death. Isaiah the prophet came to him to tell him a word from the Lord that he would die but Hezekiah prayed to the Lord to remember him and how he had walked faithfully with a whole heart so the Lord spared him and King Hezekiah lived another 15 years, even confirming this through a miraculous sign. The king of Judah wrote a piece after he had recovered in thankfulness to God telling Him that he is oppressed, asking God to be his pledge of safety, crying out for his Creator to restore him to health so that he may live.

I know that when I chose determinedly to go through with my abortion, even cutting short the holiday I was on so I could quickly go ahead with it and not change my mind, little did I realise I was acting as if I was the one who was God, choosing life, or choosing death, with no thought of my future with that child in it; indeed cutting off that whole line. Because I had come from a broken background where my sister and I came from one set of parents and then my father and step-mother had two of their own children together and we became a blended family. The thought of having one whole complete unit of father and mother with their own offspring appealed to my idealistic mind. However our babies undeniably carry some of our physical characteristics and traits and so therefore are worthy to be valued. God doesn't make mistakes! A pregnancy carried through may expose our mistakes, or rather sin, but that is not the baby's fault. Who knows what destiny your child has. She might be another singer, like Cher, whose mother went to abort her but changed her mind at the last minute. Or the baby could be like Celine Dion whose mother was pregnant with her, her 14th child, and wanted to abort except for a priest who urged the mother not to. Or maybe the baby is a boy like Justin Bieber whose mother was encouraged to abort but she chose life and instead gave birth to him at the age of 17. Or what the singer Nick Cannon who wrote a song called "Can I live?" It goes like this in verse 1:

Just think just think
What if you could just
Just blink your self away
And just wait just pause for a second
Let me plead my case
It's the late 70's, huh
You seventeen, huh
And having me that will ruin everything, huh
It's a lot of angels waiting on they wings
You see me in your sleep so you can't kill your dreams
Three hundred dollars that's the price of living, what?
Mommy I don't like this clinic
Hopefully you'll make the right decision
And don't go through with the knife decision
But it's hard to make the right move
When you in high school
How you gotta work all day and take night school

Hopping off the bus when the rain is pouring
What you want:
Morning sickness or the sickness of mourning?

You may have conceived a baby in less than ideal circumstances but that is not the end of the story – there is so much more than just one piece of the puzzle. It's up to you to write your own happy ending. What seems like a bad ending can become a new beginning. When my children were growing up I would read them a story of a character called Woollyfoot and at different points of the story the reader could choose what ending they would like, all about making their own adventure. Well, the reality is, that still holds true for you and me today. God has given us free will to make our own choices and He will not cut across that. He does not want His children to be like robots where we have no choice, and no say. Isn't God gracious?

1. Have you stopped to think what unique features your baby will have?
2. What path will you choose for yourself and your unborn baby?
3. What talents and giftings do you have or are evident within your family?

CHAPTER 3

Matthew 6:25

Therefore, I tell you, do not be anxious about your life, what you will eat or what you will drink, nor about your body, what you will put on. Is not life more than food, and the body more than clothing?

Upon discovering that you're pregnant your first thought could be "how am I going to raise a child on my own?" This is a valid thought however the Word of God says not to be anxious or stressed about this, about your life and that of the baby; of the basic provision of food and clothing, as it will come your way. God does supply and somehow it just all seems to work out. The kindness of strangers, friends and family. God will make a way. There's always plenty to go round.

Churches are great places as they are full of people who like to help and support and even counsel. Find the right one for you. Get linked in and you will find the support you need. Babies grow out of their clothing so quickly there's usually lots of baby clothing being given away or being sold at a minimal price, also baby furniture. Garage sales in Australia are another great source of cheap items for babies.

Some areas have neighbourhood houses or community centres who can support young mums-to-be.

Again in Australia some furniture is even given away if you are quick enough as my daughter found out to her great delight.

To be anxious or fearful means you are actually putting in more belief that you cannot provide food and accommodation for you and your baby. It all seems too bleak and negative so you contemplate giving up before you even start. Fear means

F alse

E vidence

A ppearing

R eal.

I have grappled with fear a lot in my life and understand it well. I saw a poster on my sister's toilet door many years ago which goes something like this:

YOU CAN TRUST AN UNKNOWN
FUTURE WITH A KNOWN GOD.

He knows the end from the beginning and you can trust Him. He loves you and He's a good Father who also loves your unborn baby. He even knows how many hairs are on your head and He sees a sparrow fall to the ground. He cares. Trust Him.

Sometimes the timing of a pregnancy can seem to be wrong in our own eyes. Again, it's really a trust issue with God. You might have fallen pregnant sooner than you had wanted to and it doesn't fit in with your plans. When my husband and I brought our miracle daughter Janessa home from hospital (I was 37 years old) we prayed for a sister for her (she had 3 much older brothers than her). 9 months later I had a dream I had a baby girl, then, in the dream, a few days later I had another baby girl and all I could see were these long, skinny legs growing. It was around Christmas time and I was very tired at the time and my cycle was out of whack. I was planning on doing a Discipleship Training Program the following year and my husband Peter was going to mind our baby for those 2 days per week. Well I discovered I had fallen pregnant! Even though we had prayed and I had even had a dream to prepare me it took some time to adjust to God's timing. You see, I wanted to be in control. I was 38 when I had my second daughter, Kayley. If I had left it another year I would have been 39 – I just had to trust God's timing – after all I was thankful God had answered our prayer. I can be so strong-willed at times and wanted everything to go my own way in my own timing – but God knew better.

1. When have you been determined to get your own way?
2. Have you taken matters into your hands to get what you wanted?
3. Make a list of the things that have been bothering you; now write another list of what you can see the solution might look like.

CHAPTER 4

Jeremiah 1:5 NLT

Before I formed you in the womb I knew you, and before you were born I consecrated you...

Now that just rolls into the fact that God knows everything about our baby before even one day comes to pass. Kayley has indeed got long, slim legs, lanky, whereas her older sister is quite a bit shorter in stature than her – they are very different to each other in personalities as well as in looks and they are both equally beautiful inside and out. However He knew everything about them and knows what He has called them to do.

When Jeremiah says this, speaking from God's heart now as a prophet, and coming from a long line of priests, Jeremiah was told by God that He had set Jeremiah apart and appointed him as a prophet to the nations even before he was born. Jeremiah was to be a spokesman for God. God had a specific purpose for Jeremiah and you just don't mess with God and His plans.

There is a specific plan and purpose that God has called each of us to and it is wonderful in His sight. I think of Gideon when the angel of the Lord appeared to Gideon and said he was a mighty warrior or a mighty hero. He felt the total opposite and felt that his clan was the weakest in the whole tribe. Gideon eventually "gets it" and he rises up and he and his army defeat the enemy, the Midianites, and peace was restored to the land.

God has called me to be a voice on behalf of all women who, like me, have come from painful backgrounds, who have experienced rejection in some form or other; to see them set free from their past pain to see themselves the way God sees them through His eyes of love and grace. I am also called to be a voice on behalf of the unborn who cannot speak up for themselves. Their lives count; they matter; just like yours does as well as mine. Life is precious – just ask a person who is sick or diagnosed with a terminal illness how important life is.

I love the scripture written by Paul, previously known as Saul who wrote much of the New Testament in Galatians 1:14 that "but when He who had set me apart before I was born" is here speaking of God's greater plan and vision for his life. God sees the bigger picture.

Just as He has also for your baby. How special you are to Him. He cherishes you, He calls you by name, you matter so much to Him; He longs for you to draw closer, to freely come. You have been chosen by Him – He chooses YOU and He chooses your baby which He gave to you. The dictionary says to choose means to pick out as being the best or most appropriate of two or more alternatives.

To make a choice is taking the option or making the choice between good and evil. It's the higher option, the finest, the most excellent way with the best outcome or consequences. Just as God has chosen you, choose wisely, don't live with regrets as I did, keep your baby, choose to go to full-term with the pregnancy, carrying new life within. You will have absolute peace as you make this choice, this decision to keep your baby. You may have no maternal feelings as yet but you will do, they will come. It is a natural normal thing to become a mother, indeed, I believe, the highest calling of all. God has entrusted a life for you to care and nurture, a responsibility, yes, but oh what joy and love they bring many times over. I had not particularly thought of myself as "mother material" but now, after having brought up 5 children, it has been the most rewarding and satisfying role I have every done. Hard: yes; regrets: none. I urge you, with everything within me, don't act as God in your life, let God be God and keep this little life He has given to you.

1. Have you ever done anything foolishly and regretted the choice you made?
2. Do you know what God has called you to, apart from being a mother?
3. Do you know, deep down, how much God loves you and accepts you and delights in everything about you?

CHAPTER 5

Psalm 139:13-16

For You formed my inward parts; You knitted me together in my mother's womb. I praise You, for I am fearfully and wonderfully made. Wonderful are Your works; my soul knows it very well. My frame was not hidden from You, when I was being made in secret, intricately woven in the depths of the earth. Your eyes saw my unformed substance; in Your book were written every one of them, the days that were formed for me, when as yet there was none of them.

When the two cells come together, after the mother's egg has been fertilised by the father's sperm, the rapid rate of multiplication is truly staggering and miraculous. This all happens inside the darkness and the safety of the womb and even the ultrasounds do not strictly reveal everything that is going on exactly. Only God truly sees and truly knows all. Everything is completely open to God's eyes and after all He purposed for this little one to come into being.

It would seem that God would have a book where He has written down the plans and purposes of each individual before they come to be, even before that child existed. It reminds me of Jeremiah 29:11. God has plans for us for good, not for disaster, to give us a <u>future</u> and a hope. This applies to you also. God's plans are good and they are the best plans. It is for the very best.

Now I want to take you to John 3:5 where Jesus is talking to Nicodemus who was a good Pharisee. He had all these questions to ask Jesus and Jesus answered him by saying "Truly, truly, I say to you, unless one is born of water and the Spirit, he cannot enter the kingdom of God." All souls enter into this world as babies and are surrounded in natural amniotic waters, but each must go through supernatural waters in order for them to enter into the next world.

Now just bear with me. When it's time for the mother to give birth sometimes the waters break i.e. the amniotic sac which surrounds the unborn baby. If they don't break then the doctor ruptures the sac. This is something like when a person comes to the Lord he decides to be baptised in water to display to the world that they have entered the kingdom of God. Their life has already existed since conception but it was hidden, as it were, till the time of the baby's birth or arrival. There is just so much parallel symbolism from the conception of a baby until the time when the baby is fully developed and has been born which can be likened to us, as adults, in our spiritual journey with God: first believing that He exists to maturing and developing in our walk with Him through reading the Bible and being discipled and taught accordingly, until at last the day of arrival comes and we are sharing our testimony, boldly moving fully into all that God has called us to.

In the book of Ezekiel, a man who was both a prophet and a priest, the word of the Lord came to him in chapter 16 and the strong word is against faithless Jerusalem as a warning and yet the chapter finishes with God declaring that He would establish His covenant with them. (God is faithful.) In verses 4-6 Jerusalem is likened to a baby but the words I want to emphasise in verse 6 the Lord says "Live! I said to you in your blood, 'Live!'"

I believe that this word 'LIVE!' is what the Lord would speak over you today. Live! I believe He would say to your baby "live!" It is a very strong command. Move in life, stay in life, keep in life, act in life, live in life. If you changed the word "life" to "Jesus" who is life and the author of life it would read 'move in Jesus, stay in Jesus, keep in Jesus, act in Jesus, live in Jesus'.

1. Have you been born again?
2. Whereabouts are you in your spiritual journey?
3. Do you deep-down believe that your heavenly Father wants to bless you, to give you a future and a hope, and not to take from you?

CHAPTER 6

Psalm 127:3
Behold, children are a heritage from the Lord, the fruit of the womb a reward.

The word "heritage" means "what is inherited, especially owned or handed down" meaning, in effect, God owns these babies, these children, and He is entrusting them into our care. They are a reward or a gift to us, a blessing. Yes, raising a child is hard work costing us time and money but the love and joy and laughter they give in return is incalculable; there's just no comparison.

Reader, if you are expecting a baby and you are not too happy about it; allow yourself the grace to change your perspective, to see a future with this little one being a part of your life and what that may look like. With a couple of my pregnancies the timing was just not quite right according to how I had planned for these babies to arrive. With one such pregnancy I had really wanted the baby, that was not the problem, but I had other things, good things, to do. I had so rejected falling pregnant much earlier than I had anticipated and I was rock solid in that rejection but the most unusual thing happened: even though I was only 5-6 weeks pregnant or 21-28 days past conception, I could feel what seemed like kicking several times during the day and it was annoying me and I was getting tired of it. It was like the tiny little embryo was being so insistent that he was letting me know he existed and I needed to recalibrate.

I had to think again, to have a new thought. I told my husband (it seemed absurd that this really be happening and I could not explain it) and he rebuked me and told me in no uncertain terms that he wanted this baby. This completely snapped me out of the rejection of the pregnancy with a baby on his way. I felt no more kicking until the correct time to feel movement after that. I found out later that rejecting a pregnancy can result in a miscarriage.

Now I want to say to you who are in the same situation as I was on behalf of the Lord

"I WANT THIS BABY AND I HAVE CHOSEN YOU TO BE THE MOTHER OF THIS CHILD!"

I did not automatically develop maternal feelings until later on in the pregnancy eventually loving him and bonding with him before he was even born. I am close to this son and I could not imagine life without him. He is so dear to me. However, it left me with a feeling of guilt for feeling the way that I had done which brought me to the point of forgiving myself.

God is always wanting to bless us and what do most people do when they are given a gift? They receive it. Graciously. You don't know what is inside the wrapped-up present – it could be this, it could be that; you think it might be this – but is it? From which store was it bought? Does it have all the extras, the bells and whistles?

I remember when I first held each of my babies. They looked like the most beautiful babies in the world – some of them were fair with no noticeable eyebrows and some darker wisps of hair, more like my natural colouring. And all of them were blessed to have their father's trait of long eyelashes (I thought my youngest daughter had missed out badly in that department, only to recently learn that they were just fair all along and were long like her siblings). My youngest son and daughter have similar lanky builds and my children's eye colours are slightly different variations of colour. Oh the wonder of it all.

1. Have you thought of babies as a reward from God before?
2. Or have you thought of them as a burden?
3. Have you ever wanted to have your own baby?

CHAPTER 7

Ephesians 1:4
Even as He chose us in Him before the foundation of the world. In love He predestined us for adoption as sons through Jesus Christ, according to the purpose of His will.

God chose us, He chose you, He chose your baby. To choose means to adopt, to elect, to desire, to pick. God picked you, He picked me and He picked your baby. He desires your baby to live, and to have life, even before God created this world. This is His will because there is a special purpose for this one to fulfil. How special are we? God wants us. It's just so amazing.

When I chose to have an abortion I was only thinking in the present, in fact the immediate present; I did not think of the past and I certainly did not think of the future.

Notice how at the beginning of the second sentence He says "in love". He chose us because He loves us and He is in love with us. He is a God of love and He is a good, good Father. He has good plans for each of our lives, including you, good plans. Your earthly father may have let you down but your heavenly Father will not, cannot, that goes against His very nature. He is a loving God.

God determined beforehand that we would be His sons and daughters through Jesus Christ because He desires family. Just as we, as we are growing up, and left the nest, met the right person for us and get married, we have a normal, natural longing to procreate, to start our own family. This is not an original desire but came first from God. He loves each and every one of us, a part of His creation, and He longs for us. Family matters to God as He formed man from the dust of the ground, then He built Eve from Adam's rib and they were husband and wife and they were to have their own family. When Jesus was dying on the cross and He saw His mother and disciple John, He told His mother that John was her son and told John that here is His mother. That is how valuable families and family units are to God.

We often say "well, it's my free will, you know" or "it's my choice, it's my body" but do we consider what God's will is in the matter. I have made many decisions without consulting God on the matter and it has proved to be not the best choice with unpleasant consequences that can have a long-lasting effect. I have heard it said about God's perfect will and His permissible will. Permissible will is what God allows because we have the freedom to choose even though we may sin. God's perfect will and what gives God pleasure is souls being saved and His people walking in all of His ways according to His Word. To obey God is better than sacrifice and creates peace. Peace can never be underestimated in this world we live in and the best thing we can do is to do what God says. I love what Romans 12:2b says that we are to prove what is the good and pleasing and perfect will of God is for you. If you do something wrong, there is no peace, but when you do what is right there is. If you have no peace with regards to considering having an abortion, then don't do it. I have heard of certain well-known women who have made that decision and afterward were devastated at the guilt and the emotions they felt that they ended up taking their own lives. Absolutely tragic. A double tragedy of both mother and baby and so unnecessary. God has given all of us a conscience and we must not be double-minded as I was and go against what our conscience is telling us.

1. Have you ever done something deliberately and gone against what you knew was your better judgment?
2. Do you truly realise how special you are to God and that He chose you?
3. How important is family to you and having your own family?

CHAPTER 8

Psalm 8:2
Out of the mouth of babies and infants,
you have established strength.

I have a strong maternal instinct, a mother's heart which has developed more and more. My sister had always seen herself as surrounded by little children and she ended up having five children in 5 years. I did not, at least not like that, nor could I have done so. However, we are both strongly maternal, caring, nurturing women. We were born to be mothers and I regard mothering as the highest call in my life although I did not recognise it in my teens. So for me it completely went against the grain of everything of what God had made me to be, to go and have an abortion. It was completely unnatural and wilful.

One translation says "From the mouths of children and babies come songs of praise to you. They sing of your power to silence your enemies who were seeking revenge"(ERV). Babies and children are just so innocent, so pure, and easily speak of God. When our daughter Kayley was 3 or 4 years of age I would ask her if she wanted this or that and she would go away and then come back and say "God says YES or God says NO. Now whether this was her conscience or not she already had a relationship with God which developed over the years to full bloom. God inhabits our praises and as we praise God in the midst of what is going on in our lives around us it no longer feels so bad – God somehow turns it round for good. I had the 'flu once and was lying on the sofa feeling depressed and miserable and then I had a thought that I was going to praise God out loud for five minutes. At the end of the five minutes I felt so much better and all depression was gone. It works – try it!

God is able to silence your enemies. All those who accuse you, negative thoughts making accusations, people who may mean well but perhaps are telling you to get rid of the baby, get rid of the evidence, good people even, Christian people. Do not listen to them! Listen to your heart. I thank God that you are reading this book before taking any action. Listen to your heart.

So what if you fell pregnant and you weren't ready for it, you weren't prepared. In the overall scheme of things does it really matter? Trust God and His plan for your life and now for your baby.

Life is a gift, you are unique, God has a plan, trust Him, you are chosen because you are special, babies are a reward and are a part of God's family and babies praise God just by being there.

Did you know that you are made in the image of God? That means that masculinity and femininity must therefore reside in God to complete that image. Mothers are seen as warm, caring, loving soothing, relationally-minded and aware, accepting but compassionate, gentle, affectionate, nurturers. However not all mothers are like this which can create a deep sense of abandonment or rejection. However they can only do the best with what they have experienced. You can't give away what you haven't been given – except in God. I was blessed to have fallen pregnant with my oldest child just after I really began walking with God and as I mothered my children, God was mothering me. I remembered my grandmother's example in mothering and my mother-in-law's selfless love revealing what a mother's love looked like that I could relate to.

I want to pause right here and share with you from Mark 10:13-16, one of my favourite passages of scripture: "And they were bringing children to him that he might touch them, and the disciples rebuked them. But when Jesus saw it, he was indignant and said to them, 'Let the children come to me; do not hinder them, for to such belongs the kingdom of God. Truly, I say to you, whoever does not receive the kingdom of God like a child shall not enter it.'" And he took them in his arms and blessed them, laying his hands on them.

Now I want you to visualise yourself as one of the children being brought before Jesus amongst the other children. Your eyes are transfixed on Jesus and His eyes. His eyes are so warm and engaging, so inviting, and He's looking at <u>you.</u> Just one touch from Him reassuring you of your worth even as the disciples were rebuking your group and telling you all to go away. Jesus then steps in to rebuke them, to tell them off, to instead welcome you and the other children, gathering you into His arms, full of acceptance and love, blessing you, blessing all of the children and laying hands on you. Before that He says to all present that the kingdom of God consists of children which includes I believe those with childlike hearts.

1. Do you believe you are made in the image of God?
2. Has anyone tried to control you or told you how you should live *your* life?
3. Do you believe that through God's help you could be a good mother?

CHAPTER 9

James 1:17, 18

Every good gift and every perfect gift is from above, coming down from the Father of lights with whom there is no variation or shadow due to change. Of his own will he brought us forth by the word of truth, that we should be a kind of firstfruits of his creatures.

I dreamt last night of unwrapping a gift. Who doesn't love gifts? But God has been and is giving us gifts or blessings as we know it all the time but do we recognise it when it comes? God gives us good gifts, even perfect gifts, the best kind of gifts.

It says in the Bible that Jesus came into the world and He was the light of the world, the true light, but the world didn't know Him.

I am one of those people who don't really like darkened rooms and I have to open up the blinds and curtains to let the light pour in. When I lived in Victoria in Australia on hot days people would pull down their blinds and pull across their curtains to keep their houses cool but nonetheless I just wanted to embrace the warm sunlight. When it is dark at night people can't see too well and use lights to illuminate their houses and torches to navigate passageways in the middle of the night. There is even a type of depression caused by a lack of sunlight in winter called SAD: Seasonal. Affective. Disorder. which would try to descend upon me during the many winters I lived through in Victoria until I would give myself a good talking to and change my attitude (I grew up in Queensland where there was a lot of sunshine on a consistent basis). Some people are afraid of the dark but we actually need to be more afraid of the spiritual darkness and choose the light which is right, and the light is Jesus. He is not only light but the life of the world and in Him is life; there is no darkness in Him whatsoever.

Do you understand what salvation really means? The four gospels in the New Testament: Matthew, Mark, Luke and John describe Jesus' life here on earth (if you don't own a Bible I recommend you get one e.g. New King James Version) and a good place to start is in the book of John who was Jesus' closest disciple whom the Lord loved and the book of John is full of love. Jesus chose to lay His life down to die on the cross of His own free will for you and me so that He could take our sins upon His body and in exchange give us His righteousness otherwise we could not see God because He is holy. Our salvation cost God everything, the highest price was paid, Jesus suffered and died the cruellest and most painful death on our behalf even though he was completely innocent and all this happened after Jesus felt the weight of the whole world's sins upon Himself in the Garden of Gethsemane the night before. I think of Isaiah 52:14b where it says His appearance was so marred (so disfigured) beyond human semblance, and His form beyond that of the children of mankind meaning His face and body was so bashed (they had brutally plucked out every hair of his beard) He was barely recognisable as a human being. He died for you. He chose to do this because He loves YOU so much. You are a gift to your parents and families and if you are expecting a child you are carrying His gift to you, His prize, His trophy.

You might be wondering what "firstfruits" mean. God says in Romans 11:16 if the firstfruits is holy the whole batch is also (that's US!) We are also His prize, the reason why He voluntarily went to the cross. Oh what incredible joy, it makes me feel like dancing! God longs for us. He longs for us to get the revelation that He is a personal God who loves us, who is proud of us, who receives joy as we take steps of courage and faith and wants to bless us and to receive His blessings and favour on our lives. If you're not sure if you have received His gift of salvation, say this prayer:

Father, I thank You for the wonderful gift you sent me of Your Son Jesus dying on the cross for all my sins and placing them on His body so that I may receive His righteousness. I receive all of the gift of salvation for my body (healing) mind (good mental health) soul (made whole) and spirit from moment forth because of Jesus' blood shed for me. I receive forgiveness and forgive those who have hurt me and now I make You Lord of my life. AMEN.

1. Do you really know you are His treasured gift?
2. Has anyone kept you in the dark about anything? How did that feel to you?
3. Have you fully received the gift of salvation Jesus was dying to give you? If not, why don't you make the most important decision of your life now by praying the prayer above?

CHAPTER 10

1 Timothy 4:4
For everything created by God is good,
and nothing is to be rejected...

When I was a little girl a part of me always felt rejected. My parents had a whirlwind romance and my mother had gone from a single woman to being married and less than 2 months later to expecting a baby from the honeymoon. Single, married, expecting all in 3 months. A lot of major adjustments in such a short time. Wounded people wound others, rejection breeds rejection. I liken rejection to a large tree:- the roots are hidden in the soil underground, then there's the thick tree trunk, the branches, and lastly the fruit. Perhaps you know someone who has experienced rejection and you recognise it by the fruit being displayed in their lives. They look downcast, unhappy, sad, unloved, constantly blaming themselves, or trying hard to be perfect, low self-worth. The root of rejection may stem right back to when they were conceived, maybe they were unwanted, or when they were born they were the "wrong" sex or the mother had a difficult birth. Perhaps for various reasons mother and baby did not bond at birth.

Rejection can be something that a person does outwardly to others ("don't come too close to me") or takes it onboard inwardly affecting their identity and outlook on life. If a significant person in our lives e.g.

mother or father, rejects us it affects us to the deepest core level of our being. However, there is hope. Our heavenly Father loves us and accepts us unconditionally and it was His will for you to be born and He will never cast you out as it says in John 6:37.

No one wants to feel discarded or thrown away and you are not. Not only does God want you, He wants you to want you, to like yourself, to embrace all you were created to be. We can form a wrong picture of ourselves which colours our world. There were times I didn't care much for myself and all I could see were my flaws and failings and all of the mistakes I'd made but God healed me of all of that and filled me with His love for me instead, to see myself as He sees me. There's no greater authority than God so what He says about me goes – I believe His report. Be at rest with yourself – God doesn't make mistakes. You are not a mistake, you are very much wanted and God has a place for you in this world, and for your baby.

Have you heard about GRACE? God'sRichesAtChrist'sExpense?

The root (the cause) of rejection produces the fruit of rejection which brings about self-rejection and the fear of more rejection. A great scripture from Psalm 27:10 reads "For my father and my mother have forsaken me, but the Lord will take me in."

I do not handle rejection well and when I hear words of criticism I can often mistake it for the person rejecting me. I became compliant growing up, to please my folks, then my husband, then friends and others to keep everybody happy (you know, don't rock the boat) because I thought that was my job to do so (after all it didn't matter what I felt or thought). I wasn't my true authentic self till God revealed the truth and healed me. This affected my love receptor, how I received and perceived love.

The Word of God says in Ephesians 1:6 that we are <u>accepted</u> in the beloved. If we are accepted then by God who are we to reject ourselves? It's an oxymoron – the Creator rejecting His own creation??? Impossible! But,

God's created beings can believe the lie that they are worth rejecting. May you not fall into this category.

There are four different types of love: agape, which is unconditional love regardless of faults and failings, phileo, which is platonic and refers to friendship, storge, which is the love you have for your family, your children, and close friends, and eros love which is emotional and sexual, romantic love.

May I finish off this chapter with a prayer from Ephesians 3:16b-19:-

> *May God grant you to be strengthened with power through his Spirit in your inner being, so that Christ may dwell in your hearts through faith – that you, being rooted and grounded in love, may have strength to comprehend with all the saints what is the breadth and length and height and depth, and to know the love of Christ that surpasses knowledge, that you may be filled with all the fullness of God.*

1. Have you grown up with a sense of feeling rejected in some way which has resulted in you rejecting, possibly even hating yourself?
2. A different way of putting it: do you see yourself as lovable, worth of being loved and accepted for who you are just as you are right now?
3. A good book to read is called Boundaries which puts limits on others unintentionally hurting you and enables you to truly love yourself.

CHAPTER 11

2 Corinthians 10:5
....take every thought captive....

Who knows we don't listen to every thought that pops into our minds? You are what you think! Most of us watch a lot of television which can influence the way we think so that we take on board somebody else's thought and we run with that. We usually aren't aware of that happening but those thoughts go into our subconscious. That may not necessarily be a bad thing unless it is a lie, or something that will harm ourselves or others – that's why we need discernment and wisdom. Negative thoughts e.g. fear and worry pull us down and can bring on depression. There are many people who say an embryo is just a blob, a piece of tissue, but is that really so? This little being is at the most vulnerable time of his or her life.

In Phillipians 4:8 it reads "Finally, brothers, whatever is true, whatever is honourable, whatever is just, whatever is pure, whatever is lovely, whatever is commendable, if there is any excellence, if there is anything worthy of praise, think about these things." Notice how it says in this scripture to think on these thoughts and to even fix our minds on these good, positive, true thoughts. In other words use self-discipline to train your mind to focus aright. Of course there are certain things we can do in our lives to help us to be happy and positive. A good full night's sleep makes a difference

(I hate being tired), drinking at least 2 litres of pure water a day, eating properly and nutritiously, and excersing which releases those feel-good hormones called endorphins. And let's not forget the hormones that women have to contend with although if you do all the previous, common sense things just mentioned you should find you'll be well-balanced in this area. If not you may need to see a doctor or naturopath and I believe wild yam cream is good for restoring imbalances in this area (under supervision). As a woman I know how important it is to have time out which is something I have always tried to do on a regular basis. We are so busy taking care of everybody else that we can tend to put ourselves last which I have been guilty of. However, the Bible says to love one another as you love yourself (Matthew 22:39) which was in relation to a scribe who asked Jesus which commandment is the most important. This scripture was the second greatest commandment (look up in the context in the Bible) which reveals how important it is for us to see and value ourselves the way God sees us. We are to love ourselves in a healthy manner, we are worthy of taking good care of; it is right to do so. Which brings me to Ephesians 5:29 "For no one ever hated his own flesh, but nourishes and cherishes it, just as Christ does the church." I am bringing in your thoughts about yourself, into line with how God sees you, with the truth of the Word of God, if you have been told how stupid or hopeless or ugly you are and you have believed these things and taken them into your heart and you act out of it to the point of even hating yourself. Conversely you may never have been affirmed or encouraged or told how precious and beautiful you really are so you have believed a lie instead. I put my hand up again, I have been there. I rejected myself and judged myself for things I had done wrong, blaming myself; I wasn't perfect enough etc etc.

There is no need to rush. Abortion does not solve the "problem of being pregnant." How will you cope after having an abortion? Are you willing to pay the high price of an abortion? The grief and deep regret, the guilt, the depression? Even the numbness? You may be considering an abortion as a knee-jerk rejection – now just slow down, take a deep breath, and imagine what life might look like with your young child in it. Make sure you have loving, caring, supportive people around you in that world who will be there for you. If your world does not look like that now then perhaps you need to meet a new group of friends – you may have an Aunt Mary who has always had a soft spot for you whom you can talk to, someone unbiased. Women need to talk, so don't carry this on your own. If your boyfriend/partner is the one pressuring you to have an abortion I have a question for you. Is it worth it to sacrifice the baby for the relationship, to keep the relationship at any cost? More often than not, the relationship falls apart anyway.

Love yourself, respect yourself, you are worthy of being treated well.

1. Would you describe yourself as a generally happy person or someone who gets down in the dumps easily?
2. Do you have healthy relationships with those close to you?
3. Are you guilty of putting everybody else's needs above your own?

CHAPTER 12

Psalm 27:1
The Lord is my light and my salvation; whom shall I fear? The Lord is the stronghold of my life; of whom shall I be afraid?

When a woman unexpectedly finds out she is pregnant and does not want the pregnancy it is due to a number of factors, one of them being fear. Fear of what will people think? Fear of people knowing that you have been sleeping around. Will people judge you? What gossip will go round about you? (You might be the talk of gossip but it will be short-lived till the next topic of gossip.) In my case it was "What will my father think? Will he reject me? Will he even kick me out of home?"

Everyone likes to be liked. They like to feel accepted and that they belong somewhere. That's where they even get a sense of who they are and what their identity is. Being pregnant, especially for the first time, is uncomfortable as its unchartered waters.

A really cool thing I found out the other day is that a bright flash of light is emitted at the moment of conception caused by zinc. It is the very moment life begins (look it up on YouTube).

When we have the Lord – He is our everything – He has saved us – and He has gone before us in every situation. We do not need to fear. He is our fortress and He is with us every step of the way.

When it says in Psalm 27:1 that the Lord is my light I believe it is also meaning He is our hope. He is our revelation and opens up our understanding on this matter. He delights to save us, to rescue us from all darkness into the light, the fullness of the truth on this matter. Where there is light, truth and hope, and we walk on this pathway, there is safety and peace of mind (John 10:28 NKJV). When we trust in God no one can snatch us out of His hand where there is ALL authority. Nothing can cause them to stumble. If God is for you who can be against you?

Fear can be a paralysing thing holding us to ransom. How many times have you dreaded the worst – a loved one isn't home by the expected time and immediately your thoughts race to they've been involved in a car accident, perhaps even killed. In actual fact they may have been stuck in traffic and not able to get home on time. Fear is a form of faith but in a negative way, dreading the worst.

It can be a fearful thing to discover unexpectedly that you are pregnant, and the fear can overtake you. But now come, let us reason together. If God is on your side who can be against you? Everything will work out, take a deep breath and calm down. It will all work out just fine, you'll see. Just take one day at a time. There's enough cares in the day so just get through each day as it comes.

Trust in God is a tremendous thing to have. He will not and does not ever let us down although He gets the blame for a lot of things He has no part in. God is not like our earthly father who may have promised to take you camping but it never came about and you got let down again. The promises in the Word of God, the Bible, are yes and amen, sure to come to pass – they cannot help but come to pass. Only believe.

When my daughters and I had a year long pass to a local theme park I was determined to go on each ride at least once to conquer any fear. Some rides I went back on again, even enjoying that particular ride. My oldest daughter entered a bodybuilding bikini competition to face her fear of competing and not only won the heat for her age group but she was also the overall winner in the southern hemisphere taking out another trophy. You might be surprised by what you conquer as you face the challenges in your life including your pregnancy.

1. Are you fearful of going full-term with your pregnancy and the challenges you'll face?
2. Are you afraid of what man might think of you?
3. Do you trust God enough to know that He'll see you through?

CHAPTER 13

2 Corinthians 12:9

But He said to me, "My grace is sufficient for you, for my power is made perfect in weakness."

I love that word GRACE. A well-known anagram is God's Riches at Christ's Expense. I would not be where I am today if it were not for His grace. I doubt that I would even be alive. I like to think of God's grace as His great, godly favour. Also grace must surely be linked to gratitude. And gratitude is linked to God who gave us all things which is connected to His unconditional love, even when we don't deserve it. Grace is everywhere – it's all around us and it is attached to thankfulness (2 Corinthians 4:15). As you open up your heart and thank God for every single thing… the air that you breathe, the trees swaying in the breeze, the variety of colours in the flowers, the fragrance, the hugs from your children, a friend or a stranger, a roof over your head, your legs that walk, your eyes which see… the list is endless. Write up your own gratitude journal and your eyes will be opened to see God's grace/favour all around you.

Thanksgiving is the currency of heaven (Jeremiah 33:11).

Grace is something you and I don't deserve but God gives it to us anyway. We just need to receive it. It is God's goodwill towards us. When we are weak in our own strength and abilities we look to Christ asking for His strength to carry us on and to carry us through. God is then able to shine through the circumstance, even bringing about good out of it as we look to His ability instead of our own. This is an act of faith in God to turn the whole situation around.

I have written a book called "*Reconciled From Abortion's Chains"* which describes how God met me with His grace and forgiveness in the midst of my sin and pain. My full name's meaning transcribed by a wordsmith is "refuge of grace" which points to Jesus Who is our very Refuge of Grace.

Perhaps I can describe grace through picture form. As I was spending time with the Lord recently I could see Him sitting on His throne extending His sceptre to me. I was dressed in the most beautiful peach-coloured long silk dress flowing to the floor. I had a tiara on top of my head which was tied up with a pearl band around my forehead and heavy pearl drop earrings on my ears, combined with a wide pearl bracelet encompassing my wrist. I lifted up the skirt of my dress with one hand to peer at my shoes which were of a heavenly description like being created from a jungle vine. As I touched the King's sceptre, He got up off the throne and we danced frivolously, gleefully, with carefree abandonment. I so thrilled in His presence as we danced melodiously to heaven's rhythm. I just wanted to linger there before moving into the plans of the day. This is a picture of God's grace.

God's ability overrides our inability. He is able. God is able. We could even interchange that word "power" (for my power is made perfect in weakness) for "love". God's love is the overriding thing here – stronger than the strongest current running full bore in raging flood waters, overpowering, surging, full. His love created everything around you that you can see – after all He is the Creator; He is your Creator. His love send Jesus to the cross for you; to die for you and to release forgiveness for your sins (Acts 13:38, 39). Ferocious love, ferocious power. You need God. You need His grace, His power, His love. We all do. All the time.

My Bible translation says: for His power is made complete in weakness. That means 100%. God will come through without a doubt into your situation to bring about a glorious outcome, no holds barred! How exciting! How liberating! Grace is like a special river flowing down from the very throne room of God.

We could also interchange the word "grace" for "life". Jesus was speaking to Paul and said "My grace is sufficient for you" but in effect He was also saying "My life is sufficient for you". Jesus has done it all for you.

1. Have you struggled to believe that Christ has done it all for you? That you are worthy enough?
2. Are you thankful for your life and the provision God has supplied for you?
3. Do you find it hard to experience intimacy with the Lord? Try and set aside time to spend alone with Him, even right now, find some quiet worship music, take your Bible, journal and pen and sit at Jesus' feet.

CHAPTER 14

1 Chronicles 28:20

Be strong and courageous and do it. Do not be afraid and do not be dismayed, for the Lord God, even my God, is with you. He will not leave you or forsake you.

It takes a strong person to go ahead with an unexpected pregnancy. I guess it's all in the attitude. If you think you can, you can, and if you think you can't, you won't. I am not sure if you have heard of Joyce Meyer. She is an amazing woman of God and preaches to many people, particularly women, worldwide. Her life also has not been easy and she has come through some very difficult times. One of her well-known sayings is "Do it afraid" when faced with a challenge. Just do it anyway. Go ahead. Go through with the pregnancy and if you're still not sure about the whole thing, then, when the time comes, have the baby and look into adoption. You will never regret taking a life then and you'll be actually helping one of the many childless couples out there who would dearly love to be in your situation. Sure, no denying that this path will require courage but God will be with you every step of the way. This child has a destiny as written in Jeremiah 1:5. God knew Jeremiah before he was formed in the womb the Bible says and had consecrated him as a prophet to the nations. Imagine if Jeremiah's mother, wife of Hilkiah the priest, upon discovering she was expecting a baby decided she did not want to go ahead and have her child. Where would history be without Jeremiah? He was called to be a prophet.

In Luke 1:31 an angel came to the virgin Mary to announce her imminent pregnancy with Jesus before He was even conceived. God had a plan for this Baby to grow up, to die, to take all the sins of the whole world, to be Saviour of all mankind. In Hebrews 10:7 Jesus said how he had come to do God's will as it was written of Him in the scroll of the book. Jesus was to fulfil all that His heavenly Father had purposed for Him to do that was already pre-recorded in heaven.

Are you feeling discouraged right now, my friend? Or condemned? Perhaps you are disappointed in yourself for even getting into this situation in the first place. Your boyfriend may have pressured you or you may have felt tempted by your own desires. Remember what the Word says in 1 Corinthians 6:18. God created sex between a man and a woman in the context of marriage and it has been wired into us to desire sexual relations with the opposite sex, to find sexual fulfilment and, of course, for procreation. Don't beat yourself up. We all make mistakes and hopefully we learn from them. If you come before God and ask Him to forgive you for __________, if you repent and turn away from that sin, having a complete change-around, change of heart, deciding to choose to do things His way instead of your own way, He says in the Word, that He takes that sin away and throws it into the depths of the sea (Micah 7:19). Therefore if God doesn't condemn us, and He is the highest authority, then neither should you. He loves you and He is so merciful and willing to forgive.

Right. So now we have been forgiven and cleansed from our sin which is now behind us, we need to look ahead. What's past is past. To have an abortion now would be to sin again, which is obvious I know, and this innocent baby had no say. I used to say to my children growing up that two wrongs don't make a right. But we are not taking that route. We are looking ahead, perceiving the good that will come out of this.

So now for some practical steps. You will need to see a doctor if you haven't already. Take a support person with you. If you don't know anyone then contact one of the agencies who would be willing to send someone to help (in Australia, Right to Life in Victoria, Cherish Life in Queensland, Priceless Life Centre in Brisbane). Think positively. It can turn out for good. There are many others you can contact for help e.g. social workers, doctors.

1. Have you ever done something that you thought you couldn't do? How did that make you feel?
2. What do you think your destiny is? Your child?
3. Have you felt condemned due to falling pregnant? Look up John 8:11b.

CHAPTER 15

Psalm 111:10

The fear of the Lord is the beginning of wisdom, all those who practice it have a good understanding.

What does that mean "the fear of the Lord?" It means having a healthy, reverential view toward God. In Psalm 19:9 it says "The fear of the Lord is clean, enduring forever" and Proverbs 1:7 "The fear of the Lord is the beginning of knowledge." Some translations say "wisdom". God is our Creator and He made heaven and earth and everything in it so it is of the highest importance to be open to listening from Him and respecting the truth that He knows all.

We think of fear as being an unpleasant emotion, to be afraid of something harmful or something that's going to hurt us but to fear the Lord is positive. Because He made us and purposed for us to be here, and He loves us, (our response is) He is a good Daddy and He does not want us to hurt ourselves through making wrong choices, to love Him back. As we get to know Him more and more, intimately, through reading His Word we come to understand that He is for us; He is not against us. It took me a long while to realise that and for the truth of His goodness to really sink in. I put aside my preconceived ideas due to circumstances and the hurtful things that had been spoken over at different times. Notice how "the fear of the Lord is the beginning of wisdom." When we fear God out of reverence and love then we want to obey Him; to live according to His Word. Now it can take a long or short time to become wise, it is up to us (I recommend you read one chapter of Proverbs a day). Another way to quicken the wisdom process is to read some good Christian books or listen to Christian podcasts, and make time for it. Wisdom taken onboard can save you much heartache and enrich your life, propelling it forward. King Solomon, who wrote Proverbs, had the desire "to know wisdom and instruction and to perceive the words of understanding." To know wisdom is also to have a heart that's teachable, that's open to hear and learn, then to apply and put those principles in place. We can know something but it really isn't confirmed knowledge until it has been practised out. Now that is real wisdom. Applied knowledge. Now that's good understanding.

Read books/testimonies of women who chose the path of abortion and how it ultimately affected them in the long term. Don't just think in the now but think long-term. Look at the bigger picture, the overall picture. Don't be reactive; pause, and think it through fully about the consequences of making an unwise choice. When we are young we may not perhaps be as wise as someone who is older and has experienced much, often the hard way. Be informed.

I'm not sure if you've heard of the saying "the fear of man?" Fear of man is when you place man's opinion higher than God's or even what you really believe yourself. It's when another person is placed on a pedestal and what they say goes. Don't let that happen to you, even if they're important to you or have an authority over your life e.g. a parent might be urging you to have an abortion or your boyfriend. They may mean well but you will live with the heartache of your choice for the rest of your life, deep down. God is the highest authority there is and He loves you and embraces you and His Word says He came to bring life, and life more abundantly. Keep the baby.

He loves you and He loves your baby. Make a wise choice: to fear God and to walk in His ways.

1. Have you ever doubted God's goodness and love to you?
2. Is to become wiser something you want to do to step out as described in God's Word?
3. Have you ever made decisions to please a friend or someone close because you felt pressured to do so, just to please them?

CHAPTER 16

Psalm 27:10
Even if my father and mother abandon me, the Lord will hold me close.

Ouch! That hurts! No one likes to be abandoned and least of all from those who have given us life but conceiving a child does not a parent make; it is just the start. We can biologically have children but we need to "grow" into the shoes of becoming a parent, responsible for another's life. If we ourselves are dealing with our own issues; we can still be a good parent if it is in our heart to be one; then those blessings can flow on to the next generation. Wounded people wound others without even realising it. But the profound truth is the Lord holds us close and that is the truth, the whole truth, and nothing but the truth! What a promise! If God's eye is on the sparrow and He knows when a little sparrow, part of His creation, falls, how much more attentively is God caring for us? (Matthew 10:31) He values us so much more than we value ourselves. After all, He made you – one-of-a-kind unique, no one else in the world like you nor will there ever be. You are special to God and you are special to me. My prayer is that no matter what negative things people have said to you, no matter what horrible things you've been through, that you would see and accept yourself as the beautiful person you really are. That is the truth! You may say but I'm too fat, too thin, I wear glasses, my skin is imperfect etc etc but the truth is you, the very core of your being, the real you, your heart is beautiful and acceptable and lovable and worthy of love, and being loved. Your God, your Maker, says in His Word that He loves you, so that settles it! He doesn't make junk! Pick up a Bible and read The Song of Songs or Song of Solomon for me. That is God's love letter to you. It is only 8 chapters long. God loves you and He wants the best for you. He is holding you close to His heart especially at this time in your life. He understands you and He knows you better than you know yourself. He totally gets you! So there is nothing to be afraid of. FEAR is really False Evidence Appearing Read, remember?

This is another beautiful and comforting scripture for you, my friend, from Isaiah 40:11 "He will feed His flock like a shepherd. He will gather the lambs with His arm and carry them in His bosom, and will gently lead those that are with young." You might feel as though you've been abandoned by those closest to you who have let you down or hurt you but God has gathered you in His arm which is the place of absolute authority and He is carrying you in His bosom, next to His heart, actually you are being carried in His heart and He is gently leading you. He does not force you – He is a gentle and good God; a good, good Father.

God is closer than the air we breathe. Open your eyes and look all around you. Can you see Him in creation? Can you feel Him? Can you hear Him? Tune out the banging and the clanging of this world for a time with all of its expectations and tune in to God. Take time to sit still quietly and ask God to reveal Himself to you. He is longing for you to slow down enough to pay Him some attention, to acknowledge Him and His ever-abiding presence in your life. He brings with Him true peace where you will find rest for your soul. The world craves that kind of peace where everything is about performance and results. Keep God at your centre, as your source and all will go well for you no matter what is going on around you.

Where's your focus? Is it all about what you want and how you expect your life to look like or can it be that you can trust God enough to handle your affairs and that your life might actually turn out better in the end than you even though possible? Pause and reflect on this.

1. What's your relationship like with your father? Your mother?
2. Have you felt abandoned by either or both of them in some way? How do you think this may have affected you?
3. Have you felt the Father's hand upon you, His love for you? If not, ask Him to.

CHAPTER 17

Psalm 23:1-4

The Lord is my shepherd; I shall not want. He makes me lie down in green pastures. He leads me beside still waters. He restores my soul. He leads me in paths of righteousness for His name's sake. Even though I walk through the valley of the shadow of death, I will fear no evil, for you are with me; your rod and your staff, they comfort me.

King David wrote this psalm and he knew all about sheep as he looked after the sheep in the earlier years of his life as a shepherd. During those times of caring for the sheep he saw a picture in front of him which clearly demonstrated the love of God. The sheep lacked nothing because the shepherd had it all figured out: in springtime there is an abundance of green pasture and the sheep are allowed to graze close to the shepherd's home. There is a wonderful system in Israel when the grain has been reaped, the poor come in and glean and lastly the shepherd brings in his flock to eat what has been left behind. Wilderness of Judea has grass which becomes hay in the summer. The shepherd's job is to look for pasture. If there is no food for the sheep in winter then the shepherd feeds them himself, even taking the flock to his house if there aren't a lot of them and so the cycle is complete. The sheep do not take any concern for the outward circumstances. He's going to take good care of them and He will take good care of you and me. All will be well – the Lord says take no thought of tomorrow – just rest in me, my child. The waters are still and calm, they're not raging waters. Things are not as bad as they may seem. The waters are still and pure and clean and for the sheep not only did they get their source of water from springs but also from wells and even the dew early in the morning. Food was provided as also the water. In the past if I have been emotionally troubled sitting down beside the sea on a rock provided peace and calm to my thoughts. Still water is a stabiliser centring our thoughts up again so we have strength to go to the next step. May I recommend to you to take time out and sit beside a lake, a waterfall, or the beach and if you don't live close to one of those or even the botanical gardens then google worship music. God will restore your soul if you allow Him to. The shepherd, trusted by the sheep, leads them. What an analogy to God and His people! God doesn't force us. He has gone before us and we are to follow Him but, oh, how we can trust Him. He is our provider and He won't lead us up a wrong path. He even makes our mistakes to prosper. He leads us along the right path. Ask Him to do that for you, even now, acknowledging His presence in your life.

The path you're on may seem like a deep valley, one that seems near impossible to climb out of and you may be really struggling at the moment through this valley of the shadow of death but remember:- it's just a shadow. I can see the Lord, your shepherd, turning back and He's looking straight at you. His eye is on you and His arms are stretched out, beckoning you, welcoming you and His eyes are filled with tender love for you. He believes in you. He knows you and He's there for you. He's called you to be an overcomer; He knows you're a conqueror and you'll get through this. Don't be afraid for God is with you and He is for you.

The shepherd used a rod to protect the sheep from bears and lions and other predators. At this vulnerable time you need protection; protection in your inner mind and thought life from satan's deadly and destructive thoughts and outwardly from judgments and criticisms from those near us which deeply affect us. At this point I need to pray: "Oh Lord, you love your daughter so much, your heart is filled with compassion for her and the situation she finds herself in, guard her heart and her mind in Christ Jesus, give her the strength and fortitude she needs right now, that you would keep out the harm and fill her with your goodness; lead her along your right path, in Jesus' Name, amen."

It's interesting that God uses His staff for gentle correction or re-directing. But I have discovered there is another use for the staff which was also used to draw the sheep together in intimate relationship. The staff is used as an extension of His arm. During lambing season a lot of lambs are born at the same time and it is important that the right lamb is returned to the right ewe so both are kept safe and together, hence the staff comforts or does the job it was required for.

1. Are you still troubled in your soul? Then go to the Shepherd.
2. Do you believe Jesus will take you along the right path for His Name's sake?
3. He's even prepared to lay His Name on the line.
4. Can you see the right path to take now? What does it look like? Tell someone.

CHAPTER 18

Luke 1:30 & 31, 38
And the angel said to her, "Do not be afraid, Mary, for you have found favour with God. And behold, you will conceive in your womb and bear a son, and you shall call His name Jesus..." and Mary said, "Behold, I am the servant of the Lord; let it be to me according to your word."

Who doesn't like the word "favour"? It means approval or support for someone. When the angel Gabriel showed up, sent by God, to Mary to give her a message it must have been overwhelming to say the least. She would have likely been in her early teens, maybe just a young 13 year old girl; but she had found favour with God. So much favour in fact that she was chosen to conceive Jesus even though she was a virgin. How extraordinary! God, the Creator, living inside His own creation! What is also astonishing is Mary's response – she was completely submitted and yielded to the Lord's will in her life. This was a part of their Jewish culture for women to be submissive but the consequences of being found to be pregnant when betrothed to another man was stoning to death. Mary trusted God with her very life when she said yes to God's will. Mary soon afterwards went in haste to a town in Judah in the hill country to visit her relative Elizabeth and her husband Zechariah where she remained for 3 months. Apparently it is a custom in the Middle

East to have complete rest during the first 3 months of pregnancy, the most critical phase of a baby's life. How beautiful that Elizabeth confirms the miraculous pregnancy as she was filled with the Holy Spirit as Mary enters her place. This would have been a huge thing for Mary who saw and spoke to the angel Gabriel about Y'shua Hamaschiach, the Messiah, growing in her womb. She would have understandably been tempted to be fearful but then she would remember what the angel said to her confirmed through Elizabeth.

And now you are in a situation beyond your control and it just does not seem convenient or the perfect time to go through a pregnancy, to have a baby just now? We live in a culture where it's all about self and what we want. Selfishness is the opposite of love. I think of 1 Corinthians 10:13 (KJV) "There hath no temptation taken you but such as is common to man: but God is faithful, who will not suffer you to be tempted above that ye are able; but will with the temptation also make a way to escape, that ye may be able to bear it. I used to believe that that meant at the very exact point of the trial God would come through at the last second and rescue me. Yet experience has proved that to not always be the case. The literal translation means He will enable us to endure the way out. In other words His grace will see us through and we will get through this. Big difference. There is a part for us to play. Wanting to be rescued, yes, would be nice, but we may believe we are the helpless victim whereas the reality is this too shall pass and God will get us through this time.

We look at the circumstances full in the face, seeing the truth for what it is (there's a baby on the way), take responsibility, and get on with it, all the while trusting God. He's not taken by surprise.

This baby has a right to live just like every other human being. The baby did not ask to be born – this was completely out of the baby's control. You really, really may not think you able to raise this baby. Is there a relative who would be prepared to do this? What about adopting out the baby or putting the baby into a nice Christian family through fostering? Then you will have a clear conscience. Conscience = God-given moral consciousness Romans 2:15a "They show that the work of the law is written on their hearts, while their conscience also bears witness." Conscience is that inner sense you have of what is right or wrong; how you judge your morals through what actions you take. You don't want to regret the taking of your baby's life. You can never get that decision back again and I urge you NOT to do what I did and for the rest of your life regretting what course you took. The Bible also talks about a seared conscience – I liken it to a hardened, insensitive heart turned against oneself to agree with a lie. I believe if you have got this far in reading my book that your hearts are still soft and teachable and you are searching for the truth and the right path to take.

1. Do you believe God cares enough about you and your baby to pull you both through?
2. Can you trust God with the big picture? Do you trust God?
3. Who do you know who could help get you through your pregnancy and the early days of looking after your baby? I believe there will be someone even if you have to think outside the box.

CHAPTER 19

Proverbs 3:5 & 6
Trust in the Lord with all your heart, and do not lean on your own understanding. In all your ways acknowledge Him, and He will make straight your paths.

Have you ever been half-hearted about something or someone? I have. It doesn't work, does it? You can't fully commit to them because there is a little bit of doubt and you hold something back. God is not like man (scripture says that He should like Numbers 23:19a). He can be trusted 100%. His name is faithful and true. So what does it mean to trust God 100%? I would say to abandon yourself totally to Him, including your pregnancy. Embrace God and His plans for your life even though you may not see how things will turn out. Sure, life may not currently be as you envisioned it to be, I understand that, but just like a yacht out on the water, when the wind whips up, you need to adjust your sails. You can be flexible and accommodate this growing life within. Recognise God as your Creator, the One who created and still creates, the One who made you and the new life within.

If you don't have a relationship with God, then I would highly recommend you do. Press in to God – He loves you more than any person on this earth (yes, and even your mother). Read His love letter: the Bible. It is nourishing for your body, mind, soul and spirit. It renews your mind and clarifies your thinking. All confusion goes. You will receive Godly wisdom and instruction. You will learn about the mighty acts of God and all about Jesus' life when He walked this earth and where He is now and what the future will be. If you're not sure where to start, start with a chapter from the Old Testament and one from the New Testament and a chapter from Psalms and one from Proverbs. In fact a word of wisdom here from my sister would be that if you are feeling distant from the Lord and you don't know where to start reading the Bible then take a look at your calendar and see which day it is today and start on that chapter in the book of Proverbs and keep going thereafter e.g. if it's the 6th then read chapter 6 of Proverbs etc. Spirit and soul food. My day looks a whole lot better after I have done my Bible reading for the day than if I don't. You might be wondering which Bible translation to get. Some people stick with the K.J.V. but others go for the N.K.J.V. (New King James Version) which may be easier to read and understand. My favourite translation is called the One New Man Bible, Revealing Jewish Roots and Power, which has been translated from the Hebrew and Greek texts. I just love my Bible because it is the living Word. It's alive and contains everything in it for life.

Following God's plan for our lives is so much easier and simpler than our own plans for our lives. When we do it our own way we end up in a mess with lots of bends and forks in the road behind us, but when we do things God's way, our lives somehow seem to straighten up. Looking back over my life now this has definitely been the case with me. It's not hard to make a mess of your life on your own. You don't need me to tell you this. I love the scripture from Jeremiah 29:11 "For I know the plans I have for you, declares the Lord, plans for welfare and not for evil, to give you a future and a hope." God wants to bless us, to give us a future that will be good, to have hope that it will turn out all right in the end. God has pure motives for you; He wants the best for you. He's got your back.

Read His Word. Listen to Him. Just trust the outcome – don't be afraid. Don't feel pressured by other people even if they're well-meaning, to go through with having an abortion. This is your body, your life, your baby, and you don't want to carry scars for the rest of your life because you listened and were persuaded to do something that went against everything you had believed in.

1. Have you been in a relationship with someone but you held something back because you couldn't fully trust them?
2. Do you own a Bible? Do you understand the scriptures? If the answer's NO then ask God to give you understanding before you read it.
3. Do you want to do things your way or God's way?

CHAPTER 20

1 Corinthians 14:33
For God is not a God of confusion but of peace.

Ephesians 2:17
And He came and preached peace to you who were far off and peace to those who were near.

I love that word "peace." It means "freedom from disturbance, tranquillity." Confusion is a bombardment of thoughts and this is the meaning: uncertainty about what is happening, or the state of being bewildered or unclear in one's mind about something. Finally, I cannot emphasise enough the importance of not taking any course of action, in life, that does not give you peace and you are not settled about it. Let peace be your umpire. Actions taken in haste usually never bring the right result. You truly do not want to live your life looking back with regret. Confusion is like a whirlwind and when we operate out of a confused state we are operating out of panicked emotions, and emotions aren't necessarily a good guide. I was one of those people led by my emotions until I prayed for weight and balance between my head and my heart and my heart and my head, and I pray that for you too.

A good picture of the difference between confusion and peace is of a river I walked along just last week where the water was flowing gently by, bringing inspiration and a calm to my soul. The next day or so a cyclone hit that same river flooding the banks but now the water was swirling angrily and the river was brown and muddy and unappealing. Peace is so much better than confusion. There is no price you can place on peace. Make the right choice and you will have peace in that decision.

And, as it says in Ephesians 2:17 above Jesus' will for you is the way of peace whether you know or not, His desire is for you to choose peace. He knows what is best for you after all. When I chose to go ahead and have an abortion I was stubborn and determined to have my own way but did it bring me peace? I can't say it did. Instead it brought turmoil and confusion and I internalised it so that the confusion went on the inside of me. I let the world dictate to me what choice I should make; it's called fear of man.

For thousands of years, Jews have greeted one another with a blessing, like "peace unto you" and the other person says "unto you peace". I really like the meaning of the Hebrew word "shalom." It means peace, harmony, wholeness, completeness, prosperity, welfare and tranquillity OR as my interpretation: nothing missing, nothing broken. When there is nothing missing and nothing broken there is true shalom, true peace. This is God's desire for you and that is why He sent Jesus to fallen mankind. He is the only way to peace and one of His titles is Prince of Peace (Isaiah 9:6). He is Peace itself. Shalom also means an absence of disorder so it would stand to reason that that would also include an absence of confusion.

Which path will you choose? Matthew 5:9 says "Blessed are the peacemakers, for they shall be called children of God." A peacemaker is someone who reconciles two differing parties. Jesus is the ultimate Peacemaker reconciling us to God. I used to liken myself as a peacemaker as a Mum when my children were fighting, rather like a referee. Notice in the above scripture how peacemakers will be called "children of God." They are operating out of God's kingdom. New here's a thought, how about operating out of peace towards yourself? What will give you true peace? Following God's plan for your life. He even turns our "mistakes" into joy!

1. When was the last time you felt really good about something that you experienced a deep, inner sense of peace?
2. Have you had a situation where you had no peace but you still went ahead anyway? What happened?
3. Have confused thoughts and emotions brought clarity to your life? Ask God for a "sound mind." Joyce Meyer has an excellent book out called "The Battlefield of the Mind" which I highly recommend.

CHAPTER 21

Romans 12:2
Do not be conformed to this world, but be transformed by the renewal of your mind, that by testing you may discern what is the will of God, what is good and acceptable and perfect.

Don't be moulded into the pattern and expectations of this world which is passing away as we know it. But be transformed… my oldest son growing up loved using his imagination with various figure men and one such game he played was transformers where alien robots were transformed or changed into machinery in the battle between good and evil. In the verse above it says to be transformed (or changed) by the renewal of your mind. My One New Man Bible says it like this "but you must from the inside continually be changed into another form, by the renovation of your mind." In other words allow your mind to be renewed which is an absolute necessity. This comes about by reading God's Word, receiving sound Biblical teaching, being disciple through a loving Christ-centred church, attending Bible studies, having a Godly mentor and friends etc. Be hungry to seek out all that God has for you which will take the rest of your life as you know it here on earth. I have been a Christian for almost 40 years and I am still learning and still growing and yes still having my mind transformed and renewed. It is an ongoing work in progress. Stay teachable. Don't ever think you have "arrived." We are a work in progress.

Discernment is a wonderful God-given gift. But notice how it comes AFTER the renewing of the mind. To discern means to have the ability to really see things as they are in the light of God's truth. I have made a few mistakes in the past where I have not accurately discerned situations in the light of truth, but acted out of my emotions, a bit like the frog in the pot of water which is gradually heated up, not discerning that the water was getting hotter until it was almost too late. I learnt the hard way causing myself and my family grief along the way, which didn't have to be if I had been discerning, seeing outside the situation as God saw it.

If you are still reading this book and you are still pregnant and you have decided to keep your baby then this book has done its job. You have learnt from my mistake, your mind has been transformed and renewed and changed, and you, like the frog (please excuse the pun) has just jumped out of the hot saucepan. I am so happy and relieved for you. You know what God's good, acceptable and perfect will for your life is in your situation. Now stay on His path for your life for your sake and that of the baby's. Seek to be Jesus' disciple.

I want to close with a prayer of blessing over your life and the little person you are carrying:

> Dear heavenly Father, you intimately know the life of the reader _________ and you know all the circumstances in her life and what has brought her to this point. You love her SO much and have already forgiven her through Christ Jesus her Lord. You understand her thoughts and you know all her ways (Psalm 139:2 & 3). Your hand is

upon her (verse 5). Your hand leads her and your right hand (of authority) will hold her, will keep her (verse 10).

Lord I pray Psalm 139:1-18 for this precious woman, that you would possess her thoughts (verse 13) and she would see how truly valuable and of great worth she is to You, to herself and to others. She is <u>altogether</u> lovely. I pray that she would perceive herself in the way in which you do. (You are IN LOVE WITH HER.)

I also pray for all confusion to be broken off her mind, all chaos and disorder to GO, in Jesus' Name, and for your overwhelming, overtaking peace to flood her entire being, body, mind, soul and spirit.

Heal her heart, Lord, mend any broken places in her life, and gently restore her and lead her in the way she is to go. Pour out your oil into her innermost being. She is loved and she is lovely. Lead her in the paths of righteousness for Your Name's sake, amen.

I bless you to be all that God has called you to be in the Name of Jesus.

The End

www.ingramcontent.com/pod-product-compliance
Lightning Source LLC
LaVergne TN
LVHW050610100826
845148LV00015B/3205

* 9 7 8 0 6 4 8 8 8 7 3 1 7 *